MW00592394

American Hero

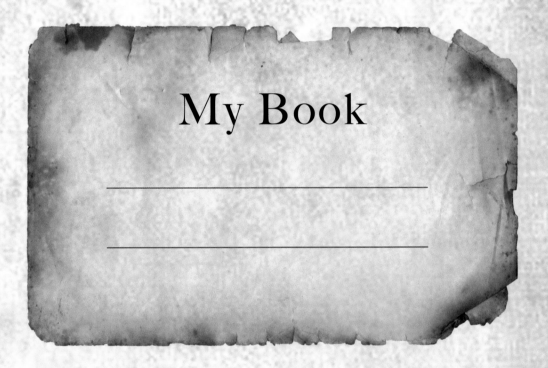

My Book

_____

_____

American Hero

John Marshall, Chief Justice of the United States

By David Bruce Smith

Illustrated by Clarice Smith

BELLE ISLE BOOKS
www.belleislebooks.com

ISBN: 978-0-9859358-6-3

Library of Congress Control Number: 2012955516

www.belleislebooks.com

FOR MY FATHER,

who was convinced that John Marshall,
the "forgotten" Founding Father,
composed a life worthy of study and
remembrance by every American.

The year was 1755. A boy was born in a small wooden cabin in Virginia. His name was John Marshall.

1755 was a long, long time ago. Life was very different then. There were a lot of trees and many animals, but not a lot of people in Virginia. There were no towns and no schools where John's family lived. In fact, when John was born, America was not even a country.

John was the first child. Then two sisters and one brother were born.

Childhood was a happy time. John woke up early and took long walks in the woods. Some days his sisters would come, too. John wanted to see a bear and trap it. He loved taking long walks his whole life.

John's father was Thomas Marshall. Thomas often worked away from home and John missed his father. John was lonely some days, but when Father was home, it was a special time. John's father taught him how to hunt and fish. John loved this time with his father.

John's father had a friend named George Washington. Sometimes, George came to their house for dinner. What great visits they had! Did you know that George Washington later became our country's first president?

John's mother was Mary Marshall. She was very pretty and very smart. In the 1700s, many women and girls could not read or write—but John's mother could do both.

Mary Marshall taught her boys to read and write—and she taught her girls to read and write, too.

"Study hard!" said John's father. The boys and girls studied hard to be a success. John's first teacher was his mother, and she was a great teacher.

John's father built a new house called
"The Hollow." The family moved when John
was seven. The new house was much
bigger. It had four rooms.
It had two fireplaces and
a huge yard.

Six more brothers
and sisters were
born at The
Hollow. Now
there were ten
children.

John heard his father talking to his friends. People were angry about how England treated them. England gave them a hard time. England was not fair. England charged a lot of taxes. People did not like England's rules. Now, it was getting worse. Many people wanted to be free from England. John's father was angry, too.

John was worried. Would they go to war? Would they fight the English? John's father said the English wanted to control them. America tried to work it out. But England was angry, too.

So, in 1775, the war began.

John and his father, Thomas, became soldiers. John was a tall, strong man, and he was a good soldier, too. Many fathers and sons became soldiers to fight the English.

On July 4, 1776, the Declaration of Independence was signed. On this day, America's leaders said, "We will be FREE! England will not rule us. We will be a new and special country." This was America's birthday and Americans were very happy. People rang bells to celebrate and share the news.

One big bell was called the Liberty Bell. Liberty means freedom ... and this was a day of freedom.

But the war with England was not over. America and England would fight seven more years before America won the war.

In 1777, John and the other soldiers had a very hard winter in Valley Forge, Pennsylvania. It was cold and snowy. The soldiers stayed in rows of log huts. There was little food. There were many diseases and little medicine. Many men died.

John Marshall tried to make things better for the soldiers. He often told stories. He made up games. He tried to settle arguments and keep the rules. John always tried to be fair. In a way, this was his first job as a judge. John never forgot that hard winter!

In 1780, John left the army and went to college. He studied law for two months and became a lawyer.

John then moved to Richmond, Virginia. He opened a law office. John was a good and fair lawyer. He was polite and kind. Everyone liked John Marshall and wanted to hire him.

John also had many famous friends. They talked over problems and tried to fix them. John helped many people. He was very busy and a big success.

John married a woman named Polly. John and Polly lived in Richmond. Polly was a good wife and good friend to John. Polly was smart, pretty, and funny.

She liked to host parties in their great big dining room. John and Polly were very happy.

*S*oon, America had problems with France. France was being a bully. France was sinking our country's ships. The President asked John to help make things better.

John sailed to France. He tried to fix the problems. John lived and worked in France for one year. But after so long, John missed Polly and his children. He wanted to come home to Richmond.

John had done a great job in France. He did not let France bully our country. After John came home from France, he was famous.

President Washington wanted John to work for America. Many more people wanted John to work for America, too. But John was happy as a lawyer in Virginia. He was a great lawyer and he did not want to be in public office... so he tried to say no. But President Washington said, "It is good for the country and you are good for the job." John could not say no to his good friend, President Washington.

It was a tough choice. But as promised, John ran for election. He was elected to Congress. Now John Marshall would help *make* the laws.

John did a good job as Congressman. He was still kind and helpful to many people. His job kept him very busy.

Many nights, John brought work home. He talked to Polly about his work late into the night. Polly was John's best friend and helped him a lot with his work.

Later, President Adams asked John to be America's Secretary of State. This was a very big job. John became a voice for America in the world.

Then President Adams asked John to be the Chief Justice of the United States. John Marshall would be perfect for this job. He was loyal and smart. He was a good thinker and a great leader.

$\mathcal{S}$o, John now became the top judge. He was now the most important judge in America.

As Chief Justice, John Marshall made new rules for the Supreme Court. In England, judges wore red robes and long, itchy wigs. In John's court, they wore black robes and no wigs. John's judges worked long hours and many days. They lived together. They ate together. The judges talked until they agreed on one view. Always, the judges tried to be fair.

John was Chief Justice of the United States for thirty-four years. John Marshall was called the Great Chief Justice. He made the United States Supreme Court strong and important. His court protected America's laws and the people's freedoms. John was very successful as Chief Justice.

ut later, things became hard at home. Polly was sick. She became sicker and sicker. She stayed in bed most of the time. John loved Polly very, very much. He helped her in many ways. He read to her. He talked with a quiet voice. He helped with the chores and went to the market. One time, he even sent a note to a neighbor asking him to quiet his dog. He hoped his Polly would get well.

Polly died on Christmas Day. The year was 1831, and she was sixty-six years old. John's heart broke. He missed Polly so much.

John Marshall still worked hard on the
Supreme Court. His job as Chief Justice
kept him busy. John also read books. He told
stories to his grandchildren. He played chess
and other games with friends. He loved his
children and family. John still missed Polly
very much.

One day in 1835, John was visiting
Polly's grave and he became sick.
John went to his doctor, and a
few weeks later, he died.

John Marshall, the Great
Chief Justice, had died.
The whole world
was sad.

John Marshall was a hero. People
wanted to honor him. They wanted to
ring the Liberty Bell for him.

So, the big bell rang at John's funeral.
All of a sudden, there was a loud sound.

The Liberty Bell....*CRACKED*.

Do you know that bell...

                    never rang again?

Reading List

How many of these words can you read?

John Marshall	Celebrate
Thomas Marshall	Together
Mary Marshall	Success
Polly Marshall	Famous
The Hollow	Hero
Oak Hill	Helpful
President	Polite
George Washington	Loyal
John Adams	Smart
James Monroe	Leader
Country	Soldier
United States / America	Lawyer
Scotland	Congress
France	Secretary of State
England	Judge
Liberty Bell	Chief Justice
Freedom	Supreme Court

Visit our website for more activities:
www.JohnMarshallFoundation.org